underwater animals

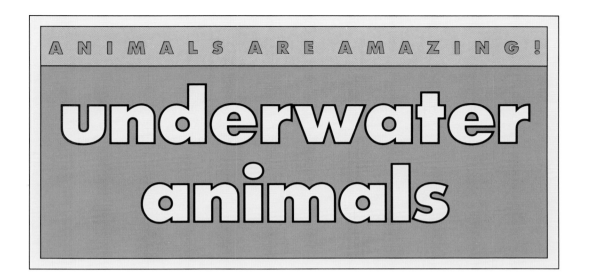

ANIMALS ARE AMAZING!

underwater animals

DAVID TAYLOR

BOXTREE

First published in Great Britain in 1990 by Boxtree Limited
Copyright © Boxtree Limited 1990
Front cover illustration and all artwork by David Quinn

Designed by Bet Ayer
Senior Editor Cheryl Brown
Edited by Heather Dewhurst
Typeset by York House Typographic
Printed in Singapore
For Boxtree Limited,
36 Tavistock Street,
London WC2E 7PB

British Library Cataloguing in Publication Data
Taylor, David, *1934-*
    Underwater animals.
    1. Marine animals
    I. Title   II. Series
    591.92

    ISBN 1-85283-315-7

CONTENTS

Imagine that one day you wake up and your hands have been changed into flippers. Where your ears were last night you now

have gills so that you can breathe underwater. *Now* you can really explore the kingdom of the underwater animals.

The killer whale has no enemies in the water. It hunts other animals like seals, fish and sometimes bigger whales. Although it can stay under water for a long time, it has to swim to the surface for air.

The blue whale is the biggest animal in the
world but it only eats very small sea creatures.
No one is allowed to hunt and kill blue whales
but some people still do.

The electric eel makes electricity in its body.
It uses this to protect itself from enemies, and
to catch other fish by stunning them with an
electric shock.

Many sea animals can make their own light. It is very dark in the ocean so the lights help the animals see their prey when they are hunting.

The octopus hunts and eats other animals such as lobsters. It hides and waits for a lobster to come near, then quickly wraps its powerful arms around it to catch it. The lobster tries to escape but it is no use – the octopus is too strong.

THE MOUTH
WITH 'BEAK'

The octopus has eight arms. Each arm has lots
of suckers to grip with. The octopus also has a
sharp beak which it uses to bite its prey.

The Portuguese man o' war is a jellyfish that
floats on the surface of the water, with its
tentacles trailing behind. The tentacles will
sting you if you touch them.

The marine turtle uses its long feet to row itself through the water. In a race it could go as fast as 20 miles an hour. The turtle eats meat and plant food.

The dolphin is a fast swimmer and is also very clever. In wartime dolphins were trained to guard harbours against enemy frogmen.

The sailfish is the fastest fish in the sea, easily winning a race against other underwater animals. It often leaps out of the water as it swims along at a speed of almost 70 miles an hour.

The shark is the most dangerous animal in the sea. It has rows of very sharp teeth and hunts seals, dolphins, turtles and even attacks man.

The whale shark is the biggest fish in the world but it is not as fierce as its name sounds. It is very gentle and does not attack man. It feeds only on tiny sea creatures.

The elephant seal is the biggest seal in the world. The male seal can puff out its nose so that it looks like an elephant's trunk.

Stories tell of a beautiful mermaid with a fish's tail who sits on a rock by the sea. Are mermaids real? No! The mermaid was probably a seal or sea cow resting on a rock after having a swim.

The pearl fisherman dives underwater to look for oyster shells. If he is lucky he might find a pearl in one of the shells.

The cone shell is a pretty sea snail with a poisonous sting. It uses the sting to kill its prey and to protect itself. It may look beautiful but it is very dangerous.

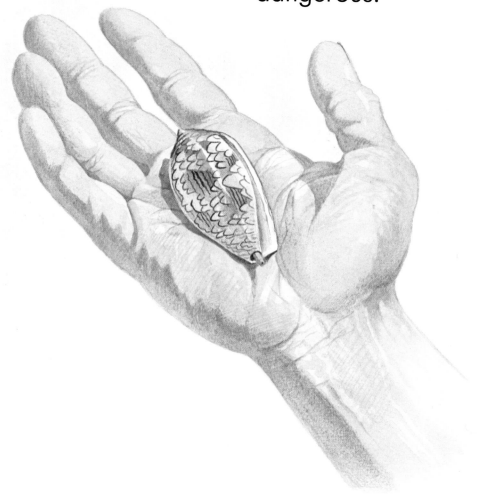

AMAZING FACTS!

1 The most powerful electric eel lives in South America – over half its body is built of 'batteries'!

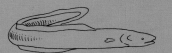

2 The tongue of a blue whale – the biggest whale in the world – can weigh up to 3 tonnes!

3 The Portuguese man o' war travels across the sea by using its body as a sail – it can float up to 6 miles per day!

4 The dolphin must have a big appetite because it has *three* stomachs!

5 The whale shark is very elusive and is only seen once every 18 months — about 115 times in all!

6 The elephant seal is a great gymnast — it can bend its backbone over backwards to form a V shape!

7 The biggest pearl ever found weighed 6.5 kgs!

8 The cone shell is a very strange creature — it eats its food with its foot!